SAPNO *Se* HAQEEQAT *Tak*

SAPNO *Se* HAQEEQAT *Tak*

Manoj Dhanda

Worldwide Published by
Pendown Press

PENDOWN PRESS LLP

An ISO 9001 & ISO 14001 Certified Co.

Regd. Office 3767A, Kanhaiya Nagar,
Tri Nagar, Delhi-110035
Ph.: 8130886000, 9650072927, 8595249536
E-mail: info@pendownpress.com
Branch Office 1A/2A, 20, Hari Sadan, Ansari Road,
Daryaganj, New Delhi-110002
Ph.: 011-45794768
Website: PendownPress.com

First Edition: 2023
Price: ₹ 640/-
ISBN: 978-93-5554-824-5

Layout and Cover Designed by Pendown Graphics Team
Printed and Bound in India by Thomson ress India Ltd.

Dedicated to My Country

This book is for my beloved India, a tribute to
our determined, unwavering, and innovative spirit.
May **'Sapno se haqeeqat tak'**
inspire fellow Indians to chase their dreams, uplift their lives,
and contribute to our nation's progress and prosperity.

Remember, you may have 1000 reasons to give up,
but you need just 1 reason to Succeed!!!

CONTENTS

About the Author

Manoj Dhanda is an accomplished author, entrepreneur, and visionary thinker dedicated to inspiring individuals to transform their dreams into reality. With a passion for personal development and a deep understanding of human potential, Manoj has empowered countless individuals through his writing and speeches.

Manoj's journey began with humble beginnings, where he faced numerous challenges and obstacles. However, his unwavering determination and relentless pursuit of success propelled him forward. From his early days as a young dreamer, Manoj always believed in the power of **TAKING ACTION** and turning dreams into tangible achievements.

Driven by his entrepreneurial spirit, Manoj has ventured into various industries, honing his skills and gaining invaluable experience along the way. Through his perseverance and innovation, he has become a respected figure in the business world, inspiring others to embrace their inner potential and reach new heights of success.

Manoj's extensive pursuit of excellence extends beyond his professional endeavors. He is a devoted family man, cherishing the love and support of his parents, brother, and wife. He takes immense pride in his sons, Shaurya and Prithav, who inspire him to continue pushing boundaries and creating a better world.

Acknowledgments

I would like to express my heartfelt gratitude to the following individuals who have been instrumental in the creation of this book and the journey that led to its fruition:

My family, for their unwavering support and belief in me. To my father and mother, whose love and guidance have shaped me into the person I am today.

- My brother whose constant encouragement and inspiration have been invaluable.
- My wife, my love, Kusum, has been a pillar of strength and love throughout this journey.
- My sons, Shaurya and Prithav, who inspire me to keep pushing forward and making a difference.
- My Mentors whose wisdom and guidance have shaped my entrepreneurial journey.
- My team at Utho, your commitment and hard work have been instrumental in the success of this mission.
- Our valued customers, vendors, partners, and well-wishers, who have believed in our vision and supported us throughout.

THANK YOU

To all the readers who have embarked on this journey with me, thank you for choosing to be a part of **'Sapno se haqeeqat tak.'** I am grateful for your trust and I hope that the words within these pages will inspire you to overcome your challenges, embrace your dreams, and reach for the extraordinary.

Note to the Reader

Dear Reader,

As you embark on this transformative journey through the pages of 'Sapno se haqeeqat tak,' I encourage you to remember the words of Dr. A.P.J. Abdul Kalam, former President of India: Dream, Dream, **Dream. Dreams transform into thoughts, and thoughts result in action.**

The objective of this book is to enrich you with the knowledge, strategies, and mindset required to bridge the gap between your dreams and reality based on my life experiences.

Remember, you have **the power to shape your destiny.** With determination and the right tools, you can turn your dreams into tangible achievements.

Take the journey, seize every opportunity, and never lose sight of your true potential.

Dream big, take action, and let 'Sapno se haqeeqat tak' be your guide.

Wishing you a transformative and rewarding experience.

Warm regards,

Manoj Dhanda

Mission
Making India Proud

At the core of Manoj Dhanda's mission is an absolute commitment to making India proud by establishing a homegrown Indian cloud provider. Inspired by the vision of Aatmanirbhar Bharat (Self-Reliant India), Manoj believes in the immense potential of indigenous technology and its ability to shape the country's future.

With a deep understanding of the global technology landscape, Manoj recognized the need for India to have its own robust cloud infrastructure. He envisioned a future where Indian businesses could leverage cutting-edge cloud solutions developed and hosted within the country, ensuring data security, sovereignty, and fostering a thriving digital ecosystem.

Driven by this mission, Manoj and his team at Utho have dedicated their efforts to building a state-of-the-art cloud platform that meets the highest standards of performance, scalability, and security.

By developing innovative solutions tailored to the unique needs of Indian businesses, Utho has emerged as a leading player in the Indian cloud industry.

Manoj's mission goes beyond mere technological advancements. He envisions a digital India that is self-reliant and capable of competing on a global scale. By fostering innovation, nurturing local talent, and encouraging entrepreneurship, he aims to create an ecosystem that empowers individuals and organizations to build sustainable businesses and contribute to the nation's growth.

Manoj believes that a homegrown Indian cloud provider not only ensures data sovereignty but also strengthens the nation's technological capabilities. By reducing dependency on foreign providers, India can develop self-reliance in critical areas of Technology Infrastructure, Leading to Job Creation, Economic Growth, and Enhanced National Security.

Through relentless dedication, strategic partnerships, and constant innovation, Manoj Dhanda strives to make Utho the torchbearer of Indian cloud technology. He envisions a future where Indian businesses, both large and small, can confidently leverage world-class cloud solutions developed within the country's borders.

With his mission to make India proud, Manoj Dhanda invites individuals, businesses, and policymakers to join hands and embrace the potential of indigenous cloud technology. By supporting homegrown solutions, India can establish itself as a global leader in the digital era while staying true to its vision of becoming an Aatmanirbhar Bharat.

Together, let us make India shine as a beacon of innovation, self-reliance, and technological prowess through the power of Indian cloud technology.

CHILDHOOD STRUGGLES

I can remember and picture those early days. My school clothes!! I only had two sets. I would wear one while the other was being cleaned. And if I ever ran off to play in my school clothes by mistake, my mother would call out to me.

I can still hear her voice, scolding me gently; her words served as a reminder of how important it was to take care of what little we had.

And if I ever ripped my clothes, I could still see my mother sitting down with her sewing kit. Her hands moved quickly, skillfully mending the tear until you could hardly see it was ever there. It was more than just sewing; it was a way of making the most we had because I only had that one set of school clothes for every day.

There are no words sufficient to describe how great my father, Mr. RamKumar Dhanda, truly was. He worked as a farmer and would go to the farmland (khet) almost every night to water the fields. This was because our town lacked electricity during the day, leaving nighttime as the only option for irrigation. Imagine those dark nights with no one else around – it was quite frightening. He put in hard work every single day. This experience taught me a valuable lesson:

when you truly need something, no matter how dangerous or scary it might seem, you'll find a way to do it. My father is the humblest person I've ever met, and I strive to be just like him.

I have fond memories of my brother, Pardeep Dhanda, and his remarkable sense of responsibility towards our family and our household needs. In our family, which consisted of two boys and limited financial resources, we relied on each other for support. We didn't have a regular income, so after he finished his education, he worked as a bus conductor. He always made sure we had what we needed. I'll never forget the time he used his extra earnings to bring home four plastic chairs and many other things. He even helped me buy my first computer when things were tough. I've always looked up to my brother for his strong sense of responsibility.

Even though times were tough, there was something special about it. It taught us to value what we had, to make do, and to find joy in the little things. Life may have been simple, but it was our life, and it shaped us into who we are today.

"In my early life, I faced many difficulties, but those challenges taught me some important lessons. I realized the power of simplicity, being resourceful, and the importance of family. My parents' love and support showed me the value of being strong and bouncing back from tough situations. No matter what obstacles we encounter, with determination and the support of our loved ones, we can overcome anything."

CHAPTER 2

DREAMING OF A BETTER FUTURE

It had always been my parents' dream that we would achieve what they couldn't, primarily through education, such as getting a stable job and a nice home. I attended a government school, but I must admit that I didn't have a strong passion for studying; for me, going to school felt more like a routine task. Consequently, my parents often found themselves worrying as I struggled with irregular school attendance and a lack of focus on my studies.

I remember our whole family - my mother, father, big brother, and I used to stay in a small room with limited resources.

I recall that when it used to rain, water droplets would enter the room, and sometimes we would place buckets to collect the water. My mother would apply a mud paste around the house to keep it clean.

Let me tell you that before we moved into that house, we used to store buffalo dung in that room, but once we started living there, my mother kept it so clean that it was astonishing.

Lessons from Dreaming of a Better Future:

Learning for YOU: Education is the key to fulfilling dreams, even with limited resources. Small steps can lead to big changes, honoring parents' hopes and creating a brighter future.

CHAPTER 3

LOVE AT FIRST SIGHT

Since childhood, I have always been fascinated by electrical devices like TVs, radios, and anything else you can think of. You could say I wanted every gadget.

I had a strong desire to understand how each gadget worked. I'd often open up our TV or radio just to see what was inside.

Instead of going out to the fields, I remember staying at home, opening up our TV, and finding so much happiness in that. It felt like the best thing I could be doing, far more interesting than any other task.

When our TV was unavailable, my next stop was always our neighbors' place. Every day, I'd be over at their house, glued to their television. Sometimes I'd even stay late into the night. This made my parents worry. They'd be at home, concerned about us kids always going out to watch TV, especially when it got late.

Even though they were concerned, they unknowingly encouraged my curiosity. The times I spent exploring and discovering how things worked weren't just fun. They were the first steps in my journey of learning, a journey that began with a simple fascination for how things work. The joy and excitement of those times still remind me of how much there is to discover and how each of us has the potential to learn and create.

Remember, curiosity and passion can be the driving forces behind our personal and professional growth. Love your interests and let them guide you towards a purposeful and fulfilling life.

CHAPTER 4

JUGAAD!!!

In those days, owning a television was considered a luxury, especially in our humble village. Despite the struggles, my family managed to bring home a black and white TV, our first ever. It was a simple device, but to us, it was a treasure. Just across our small dwelling, our neighbors had a color TV, a spectacle of modern technology that often left us in awe.

Around that time, there was a clever invention making its rounds—a colorful cover that could make a black and white TV appear as if it was in color. The idea fascinated me, and we decided to bring one of those covers home.

We carefully placed this cover in front of our black and white TV. With each passing moment, our humble television started looking less like an old black and white model and more like a fancy color one. It wasn't perfect, but it was as if we had brought a bit of that color television magic into our home.

One memory that stands out from those times was the color TRAI - the three distinct stripes resembling our national flag, each a vibrant hue of saffron, white, and green. Every time we switched on the television, the sight of these vibrant colors from our makeshift color TV filled the room with a unique sense of pride and joy.

Despite not having a real color TV, it felt like we had achieved something special. We turned our black and white TV into a source of colorful entertainment. It was a small thing, but it taught me a valuable lesson: we can always find creative ways to make the best of what we have. This was not just about creating a semblance of color TV. It was about finding happiness and feeling satisfied with our means.

"In a world of limited resources, we painted our lives with vibrant ingenuity. Our makeshift color TV taught me that true joy lies not in what we lack, but in the art of making the best of what we have."   **- Manoj Dhanda**

CHAPTER 5

FAN OF "FAN"

As a child, I had a knack for tinkering and creating, probably a side effect of growing up in a quiet village where the hum of modern city life was replaced by the natural sounds of the countryside. In our village, resources were limited, and one such resource was electricity. It was a luxury we didn't have regular access to, but rather than seeing this as a disadvantage, I saw it as a challenge to overcome.

One day, while playing with an old radio the motor inside it caught my attention. It was just a small spinning motor, but my curious mind saw potential in it. An idea sparked in my mind as the summer heat settled in. Due to unavailability of electricity sometimes, we didn't have a working fan in our house, and the afternoons were particularly hot. I thought, "Why not use the motor to create a fan?"

So, I set about crafting a fan using the spinning motor. I found a torch with a working battery in our house. It was a simple device, but it was powerful enough to drive the small motor. I connected the battery to the motor, and to my delight, it spun, creating a gentle breeze. I had turned the regular spinning motor into a functional fan, and I felt incredibly happy about it.

From that day onwards, whenever the heat became unbearable, we would run that fan. It wasn't much, just a small breeze against the scorching heat, but it was a relief. And the reactions from others were priceless. They would look at the fan, feel the cool air, and ask, "Wow, what are you doing? This is amazing!"

Their words were not just admiration. They were fuel to my budding passion for invention and innovation. I wasn't just a kid playing with random parts. I was a problem solver, a creator who used what was available to make life better.

And that, for me, was a spark of joy and a spark of purpose. It wasn't about making something out of nothing. It was about finding a way to make things better, despite the odds. It was about showing that even with limited resources, we can still come up with solutions, big or small. It was a valuable lesson that I carried with me through life - the power of innovation and creativity, the magic of turning the ordinary into the extraordinary. And, above all, the belief that anything is possible when you put your heart and mind into it.

"I discovered the extraordinary in the ordinary. The makeshift fan became a symbol of my unwavering belief in the power of innovation. It taught me that limitations fuel creativity and that with heart and mind aligned, anything is possible."

- Manoj Dhanda

CHAPTER 6

1 > 0

Looking back at my early years, I clearly remember how things were back then. We lived in a village that was far away from the big city.

Our TV antenna was our window to the outside world. Every day, we would adjust this antenna, trying to catch the best signal or switch to another channel. It was a daily routine.

Then, one day, cable TV arrived in our village. It was an exciting day, watching the cable TV man arrive with wires and strange-looking boxes. Cable TV promised many channels, and I wanted to see them all. However, we didn't have enough money for this. I learned from my childhood that small efforts pay huge dividends.

Not willing to give up, I came up with an idea. I took a thin wire and used it to make my own cable, determined to find a solution. Suddenly, I was able to watch all these channels that we couldn't afford before, and the joy it brought was immeasurable.

When the cable TV technician found out, he couldn't believe it. He was surprised that I had found a way to watch the channels without paying, and he admired my resourcefulness.

But for me, it wasn't just about the channels. It was about showing that even when things are tough, we can find ways to make them better. It was a lesson I carried with me as I grew up - that curiosity and a little bit of clever thinking can open up new possibilities. It taught me that when you really want something, you can find a way.

In my village days, we longed for more TV channels, but couldn't afford cable TV. With some ingenuity, I made my own cable and unlocked a world of possibilities. A lesson I cherish: curiosity and cleverness can lead to solutions, no matter the circumstances.

CHAPTER **7**

THE DISCOVERY
OF TALENT

As days turned into weeks, I found myself becoming more and more interested in electronics. I began to spend more time at the local cable TV office, a place filled with fascinating gadgets and busy people.

One day, the team at the office was struggling with a tough task. They were trying to set up some channels using a big dish antenna, but they were having a hard time. From the rooftop, I quietly watched them, trying to understand what they were doing and where they were going wrong.

When they finally gave up and left, I decided to give it a shot. I had been watching them carefully, so I knew what they were trying to do. I started to repeat their steps, but with a little bit of my own twist. To my surprise, it worked! In just a short time, I had the channels set up and running.

When they returned and saw what I had done, they were shocked. They asked me how I did it, and all I could say was, **"It was easy"**.

That was a turning point for me. From then on, any chance I got, I would be at the cable TV office, eager to take on more tasks. It was exciting to learn new things and to figure out how to solve problems. The office had become my personal playground, a place where I could feed my curiosity and grow my skills. It was no longer just an office—it became a place filled with discovery and excitement, where I could dream big and make those dreams come true.

Cable TV Dish Antenna

As I explored electronics, I encountered a challenging task at the cable TV office. Watching closely, I took a chance, solved it, and unlocked a world of learning and growth. This turning point became my playground of discovery and achievement.

CHAPTER 8

A 10TH F.A.I.L

School studies and I were not best friends. In fact, I struggled so much that I failed my 10th-grade exams. But that didn't get me down. Instead, it gave me a chance to try something different.

I started learning through what we call 'open education.' This way, I could study for my 10th, 11th, and 12th grades while also preparing for competitive exams. I liked it because it allowed me to learn at my own speed and in my own style.

I had big dreams in my heart. I wanted to do something great in life but I wasn't sure how to get there. So, I followed what many people did. I joined a coaching center to study for competitive exams.

This was a common path, one that many people took hoping to reach their dreams. Was I absolutely sure it was the best path for me? Not really, but sometimes, you have to take a chance and see where the road takes you.

Even when things got tough, and my path had many twists and turns, I kept my dream alive. I believed I could make a difference. I believed I could shape my future. I believed I could achieve great things. This belief was my fuel, pushing me to keep going, to find my path, and to never stop learning.

School was a struggle, and failure hit hard, but it led me to open education. With big dreams in my heart, I followed an uncertain path, holding onto belief and determination, determined to achieve greatness.

CHAPTER 9

ZONE OF GENIUS

The place I loved the most at the coaching center was their computer lab. Imagine a room full of computers, each screen glowing like a lantern in the dark. This was my favorite spot.

Day or night, you could always find me there. It was like I was on a grand adventure, exploring each computer as if it was a hidden treasure chest.

When I was in the lab, time just seemed to fly by. It felt like I was in a magical world where hours felt like minutes. I was learning, for sure, but it was more than that. It was like being on an exciting journey, filled with new things to see and discover.

To me, the computer lab wasn't just a room with computers. It was my own special place, a secret hideout. It was a place where I could challenge myself each day, learn something new, and then come back for more the next day.

Those days in the computer lab were some of the best times of my life. I was like a sailor on an endless sea of knowledge, and each new discovery was like finding a precious pearl. The thrill of learning, the joy of discovery - it was all a part of this timeless journey that I was on. In the glow of those computer screens, I found my passion, my purpose, and a love for learning that has stayed with me ever since.

The computer lab was my special spot, where time flew by as I explored a sea of knowledge. Each discovery felt like a treasure, igniting my passion for learning.

CHAPTER 10

THE MOST IMPORTANT DECISION OF MY LIFE

I had somehow passed the competitive exam, but the score I got was only enough for a course in fashion designing. It was at this moment I found myself standing at a crossroad. The path that lay before me was not one I wished to take.

Deep down, a small voice whispered, "It's time for a change. Time to listen to your heart, to follow your true passion for computers." This was not just a faint whisper anymore; it was a compelling call that I couldn't ignore.

I simply couldn't let go of my love for computers. The excitement and joy they brought me were unmatched. It was clear to me what I had to do. I decided to answer that inner call, to follow my heart, my passion.

Gathering my courage, I shared this decision with my family. I told them I wouldn't be going for fashion designing. It was a tough talk, but an important one.

I want to share this message with you, my readers: Follow your heart. Listen to what it's telling you. Embrace what you love.

Changing your path might be scary, but doing so can open up a new world for you. The life you've dreamt of can be yours.

So dream big, chase your passion, dare to step off the usual path and make your own. When you dare to change your path, you have the power to change your life. Let your passion be your guide, let your heart lead, and you'll find that the life you've always longed for is within your reach.

After passing the competitive exam, I faced a crossroad. A strong inner voice urged me to follow my passion for computers, and I knew I had to embrace this change. I chose to listen to my heart and pursue what truly made me happy. My message to you is simple: Follow your heart, chase your passion, and dare to change your path. It can lead you to the life you've always dreamed of.

CHAPTER 11

THE JOURNEY TO AMBALA AND THE FIRST COMPUTER

I finally shared my dream with my family - I wanted to learn more about computers. A while later, I found out that one of our relatives, who was studying in Ambala, had a friend with a computer in his hostel. My heart skipped a beat.

I got in touch with this friend, and he kindly agreed to let me use his computer. The happiness I felt was like a rush of a cool breeze on a hot day. It was as if everything was starting to make sense, like the pieces of a puzzle coming together. With friends from my coaching days studying at the same college, it was like I found a treasure chest. It was an opportunity I simply couldn't let slip away.

So, I packed my bag with DVDs. Some had operating systems on them, while others were filled with software I had been studying and experimenting with. And with this, I set off for Ambala. My pocket was light, money was tight, but my hope was boundless, like the vast sky. I believed I would find what I needed there – food, clothes, and a place to stay. But most importantly, I was ready to chase my dream.

Once I reached, things seemed to line up. I shared a room with my friends, we had meals together, and whenever they left for their classes, I would often join them, jumping at the chance to use the computer.

Life was simple, revolving around the thing I loved most - computers. I was a young man with a big dream, ready to take on the world with nothing but the clothes on my back and a heart full of passion. I was open to risks, ready to step into the unknown, all in pursuit of my love for computers. Each day was a fresh start, a new chance, and I welcomed it with open arms.

Looking back, those were the moments that shaped me. They were the days when I found out what I was truly capable of, how far I could go if I really set my mind to it. If you're reading this, always remember, your dreams are worth chasing. Don't let anything hold you back. Be brave, follow your heart, and let your passion guide you. Because when you do, you'll see that the life you've always dreamed of is within your reach.

Follow your passion, grab opportunities, and chase your dreams fearlessly, for they can lead you to the life you've always dreamed of.

CHAPTER 12

LEAVING LONELINESS BEHIND

After a while, however, I didn't feel good. I felt like I was merely tagging along with my friends, not adding any value to our group. I was just there, living under their roof, relying on their earnings, and that didn't sit well with me. I felt as though I was constraining my own potential and depending on the sweat of their brows.

Summoning with courage, I decided to reach out to my brother. I wanted to be a contributor, not just a receiver. When he picked up the phone, he could sense something was different in my voice. He asked me why I needed money, so I poured my heart out, explaining how I was feeling and the changes I needed to make.

Understanding my situation, my brother sent me the money I asked for. With his support, I found myself a new place to stay, sharing a room with another friend. Now, I wasn't just a guest anymore, but a contributing member.

It was a small step, but a significant one, towards self-sufficiency and independence. It was the moment I started not just to dream, but to take responsibility for my dreams. It was the beginning of my journey towards self-reliance, a lesson that would stay with me for life.

When you're chasing your dreams, remember it's not just about reaching your destination. It's also about the journey, the lessons learned along the way, and becoming a better version of yourself.

Learn to be proactive, take charge of your dreams, and go for independence, as it's the journey that molds you and brings true fulfillment.

CHAPTER (13)

TOUGH TIMES NEVER LAST, TOUGH PEOPLE DO...

During those times, a morning paratha would often be the only thing I'd eat all day. I'd make it last, hoping it would be enough till the night. Each morning, having that simple meal made me feel like I had everything. But as the day went on, the worry would start - "What will I eat tonight?"

Sometimes, I'd go with friends to eat outside in a food-only PG for a meal, but there were nights when I had to sleep with an empty stomach. I can still remember sitting alone in my room, tears rolling down my face, my mind full of questions.

"Why am I here?"

"What have I done?"

"Is this even worth it?"

"What will I do if I go back home?"

"How long can I keep asking my family for financial support?"

These thoughts made my heart heavy, and it seemed like there were no answers.

Yet, it was during these hard times that I found the strength inside me to keep going. It was time to take action, to change my path. Thus, with a strong heart, I started looking for a job. It was a tough time, but it was these tough times that showed me how strong I could be, to change my future and keep going after my dreams.

In difficult times, I discovered the strength within. With a determined heart, I faced my worries and welcomed change. Through challenges, I found my inner power. So, always remember, when life becomes difficult, you have the ability to shape your future and pursue your dreams.

MBA of Success at the Age of 16

In the same city that had pulled me in with the promise of a bright future, I found myself taking a different path. A local outlet, a small hub buzzing with telecom services, and offering products like STD and PCO connections, became my new daily haunt.

I was barely 16, still figuring out life, and here I was, involved in a hustle that was miles away from the world of computers.

Day by day, I roamed around different neighborhoods, knocking on doors, meeting diverse people, my young hands clutching onto flyers and application forms, trying my best to convince people to sign up for these telecom services. My job was to sell, to make people believe in the value of what I was offering.

This was raw salesmanship, nothing sugarcoated about it. It was something that people usually go to business schools to learn MBA. They would sit in air-conditioned classrooms, read from glossy textbooks, and listen to professors talk about expound theories and strategies. But here I was, a teenager thrown into the deep end. I was learning the art of sales on the streets, face-to-face with real customers, real rejections, and real victories.

The money I started making was not a fortune, but it was my own. Every single penny earned felt like a pat on my back, a small victory lap, a silent testament to my hard work and perseverance.

However, as the weeks rolled into months, there was a worry growing within me.

Late at night, after a long day of work, I would sit in the dim light of my room, I found myself confronting the tough questions. "Is this where I belong? Is this path leading me towards my dreams?"

It was hard to admit, but I knew the answer was no. The world of selling telecom services was not where my heart truly belonged. I decided it was time for a change, a return to the world of computers, to the journey back towards my true passion.

It was time to return home, to start afresh.

Key takeaway for YOU: "Even though life led me to sell telecom services, it taught me valuable lessons about hard work and determination. Yet, deep down, I knew my heart belonged to computers. Hence, I made the courageous choice to return to my true passion, starting a fresh journey towards my dreams."
- Manoj Dhanda

CHAPTER 15

A Journey Back Home

After returning home, I found myself again working with telecom services. This time, it was at a nearby distributor for the same company I had worked with before, but there was one significant difference - they had a computer. I had to work to pay for my computer time, but I didn't mind. Despite earning a modest sum of 3,000 rupees a month, what mattered more to me was having access to a computer again. My heart was filled with excitement, and it was the joy of being around a computer that kept me going.

Soon, I started making my mark. People around me began to notice, appreciating me for doing tasks they found tricky. I felt like I was on cloud nine, with my days filled with continuous learning and growing. I was like dry land, soaking up every drop of knowledge that fell my way.

The work also gave me exposure to the call center industry. I started sharing my insights with them, teaching them things they hadn't known before. This exchange of ideas soon gave birth to friendships, and some of them even suggested that I join their team.

With a sense of hope and a spring in my step, I went to Sonipat for an interview. I was answering the questions confidently, feeling positive about the process, but when they asked my age, the truth – that I was only 17 – came crashing down. They appreciated my skills but asked me to return once I turned 18.

With a heavy heart, I headed to my friend's house nearby. As I sat there, I began to ponder over my next move. It was then that another opportunity caught my eye – working with a dish TV company. It was similar to what I had done in my childhood with a cable TV operator, but this time, it was about learning things from Dish TV's internal systems not as a consumer or provider and best part is... it was exactly the computer job I'd dreamed of, but it was a step into the world of advanced technology.

After returning home, I found myself working with a nearby telecom distributor, and they had a computer. Despite the modest pay, the joy of being around a computer kept me going. My dedication and skills soon earned recognition, opening doors to the call center industry. Though one opportunity didn't work out, I took a new chance to work with a dish TV company, stepping into the world of advanced technology. - Manoj Dhanda

CHAPTER 16

BREAKING THE COMFORT ZONE

With my new job, I had the comfort of living at home and sharing meals with my family. Those were simple times, but they hold a special place in my heart. Every Sunday, my mother would serve me namkin rice with curd, a humble yet delicious dish that became a symbol of our family's love and togetherness. Even today, when we get together, we make sure to relive those memories by sharing a meal of namkin rice.

As I continued to work with the dish TV company, my knowledge expanded. With every passing day, I found myself learning more about computer systems and software, peeling back the layers to understand their intricate workings. The more I explored, the more I realized the common patterns underlying different technologies.

Every software, regardless of its domain, followed a certain logic, a flow. Once I understood this, it was as if a veil had lifted. I could see the unity in diversity, the shared heartbeat of different technologies. I was no longer just a worker in a dish TV company; I was becoming a tech enthusiast, a problem-solver, an innovator.

After about one and a half years of this learning and growing, a feeling of restlessness started to stir within me. The walls of my home, as comforting as they were, began to feel a bit too close. It was time for a new adventure, a new challenge. And so, with a mix of excitement and nervousness, I decided it was time to spread my wings and leave home.

Family's love and togetherness, cherished in the taste of namkin rice. As I explored the tech world, unity in diverse technologies revealed, becoming an enthusiastic problem-solver. I spread my wings, ready for new adventures beyond home.

CHAPTER 17

A Journey to Achieve Greatness

There was a fire burning in my heart, a deep desire to do something big. The day I was leaving my home, the air was thick with emotion, and the weight of my family's love and expectations bore heavily on me

My family was trying to smile, but their worry-filled eyes were enough to reveal their true feelings. Their words of advice were ringing in my ears - "Itne bade sehar me ja raha hai, beta.. Apna dhyan rakhna."

(Be careful in the big city, son. Look after yourself.)

With a small bag of things and a little money in my pocket, I was all set to step outside our home. It wasn't easy to see tears glistening in my family's eyes, but I understood the importance of this journey.

I had to do this for them and for myself.

As I walked out of the house, I made a promise - **I would only come back when I had achieved something big in life, something that would make them proud.**

And with that promise, I set off on my journey. I had so many questions in my mind.

How will I do this?

What should be my next step?

How will I make my dreams come true?

Yes, I was stepping into the unknown, full of doubts and fears. But among all these questions, there was one thing that was clear - my determination.

My will to succeed was stronger than any doubt, any fear.

This determination, this inner strength was guiding me. It was time for me to start my journey and carve my own path, one step at a time, in pursuit of my dreams.

With fire in my heart and determination as my guide, I left home for a big city, carrying dreams and hope in my bag. The journey was unknown, full of doubts, but I promised to return only after achieving something big in life. Step by step, I carved my own path, fueled by unwavering will to succeed.

CHAPTER 18

STARTING FROM SCRATCH IN A NEW CITY

Stepping off the bus, I found myself standing in the heart of Rohtak; the big city felt like stepping into a new world. I didn't have much money and no job yet. I was a newcomer, lost in the crowd but armed with a strong will to succeed.

Soon, I stumbled upon a chance in an unexpected place - the world of the stock market. A stock market company offered me a job. It wasn't in my dream field of computers, but it was a start, so I took it.

My work at first was simple - making sure the computer systems were set up right and running smoothly. But as days passed, I started taking on more responsibilities. I was helping with placing stop losses, giving advice, and little by little, I was getting into the world of stock trading.

Yet, as I worked more, a feeling began to grow inside me. I felt like something was missing. I had left my home with a dream to do something big, but here I was, doing the same thing every day.

This made me realize something - if I really wanted to do something big, to really make a change, I had to start my own thing. I had to step out of this daily routine and make my own way.

This thought lit a new fire in me. I was ready to turn my dreams into reality and to establish a name for myself. I knew the road ahead wouldn't be easy, but with hard work and determination, I could make it happen.

Ab kuch apna karna hai - Kuch Bada karna hai.

Stepping into the big city, armed with determination and a job in the stock market, I felt a spark of realization. To truly make a change, I had to start on my own. With a new fire inside, I was ready to carve my own path, work hard, and make my dreams a reality.

CHAPTER 19

A Million Dollar Investment

One evening, I called my brother. "Bhai," I said, "I need some money. I want to buy my own computer."

I was very clear in my heart. I wanted something more. I wanted my own computer to learn, explore, and grow.

My brother, who had always stood by me, agreed to help. One of his friends had an old computer and was ready to sell it for 5000 rupees. That was a lot of money, but the opportunity it offered was even bigger for me.

So, I started my journey to get that computer. I was filled with joy. It felt like a kid eagerly waiting for his birthday gift. This wasn't just any computer. It was my ticket to the world of knowledge, to a future where I could create something of my own.

Now, I wouldn't be stuck with a regular 8 to 10-hour job just to work on a computer, I could dive deep into the computer world whenever I wanted. I didn't have to look here and there for a computer as I did for the past few years.

This was a big step for me. After many years of using other people's computers, finally, I was going to have my own. This was more than just a machine.

It was my freedom, my hope, my chance to change my life.

Every new day brought me a step closer to my dream. A dream of a world where my passion wasn't just a hobby but the center of my life. As I walked this path, I realized how strong we can be, how big our dreams can be, and how much we can achieve if we simply don't give up.

One evening, I made a decision - to buy my own computer and go on a new world of learning and growth. It wasn't just a computer; it was my freedom and a chance to change my life. As I pursued my dream, I learned the power of determination and the incredible heights our dreams can take us to if we never give up.

CHAPTER 20

JUST DO IT!!!!

My very own computer. Now, there were no limits. I had the power to chase my dreams, my way. It was like the universe whispered, "You can now do whatever you want." That's when the idea sparked, the idea to create my own websites.

But the journey wasn't easy. There were mountains to climb and rivers to cross. Creating websites from scratch was a big challenge. But challenges are just opportunities in disguise, right? I was ready to take them head on.

Hours turned into days, and days into nights. My room became my world, and the glow of the computer screen served as my sunshine. I was on a mission. Day after day, I would sit in front of the computer, eyes glued to the screen, fingers dancing on the keyboard. It was hard, demanding, but I knew it was worth it.

I was just 18 years old, and this computer was my best friend, my teacher, my guide.

That's when I realized the power of three simple words - "Just do it." I learned that action speaks louder than words. I learned that if you want to reach the stars, you must take the first step. I had taken mine.

So, dear readers, if you ever found yourself in doubt, remember my journey. Remember the power of "Just do it". Remember that when you believe in yourself, you can turn your dreams into reality.

"Just Do It', explore the universe within you, take the bold step to turn dreams into reality, for you are the architect of your destiny."

- Manoj Dhanda

CHAPTER (21)

CHALLENGES AND WINS

After a full month of hard work, I finally built my website. I had created everything from scratch and felt proud of my achievement. But, just like climbing a mountain, reaching the top was only half the journey.

Once the website was up, it started encountering problems. Unsure of what to do, I sought help. Unfortunately, the hosting providers, the people who were supposed to have the answers, left my questions unanswered.

This was hard and lonely, but I didn't give up.

I decided to learn and solve the problems on my own. I started understanding more about how hosting works. It was tough, but I enjoyed it. It felt like this was the right thing for me to do.

But then, I realized that passion alone was not enough. I was in a new place and needed money to sustain myself.

My journey had just begun, and I knew it was going to get even harder.

This is not the end, my friends. In the upcoming chapters, I'll share with you how I faced these challenges.

You will discover how I managed to keep going and found a way to make money while doing what I love.

"Meet challenges head-on, learn on your own, and combine passion with practicality to find success in what you love."

- Manoj Dhanda

CHAPTER 22

YOU ARE NOT ALONE

One thing I'll never forget from those challenging days is Sharma Ji's small dhaba (eatery). It was located by the roadside, where I could get a plate of food for just ₹ 25. However, money was tight, so I managed to negotiate it down to ₹ 15.

Even when I didn't have that, Sharma Ji would let me eat and pay him later. His kindness made me feel like someone up there was watching out for me.

Now, I have acquired the skills to solve every problem related to websites and hosting.

Next, I needed money to survive and move toward my dreams. Speaking with a hosting provider gave me an idea.

He suggested I try reseller hosting, where you buy hosting services and sell them to others. It was a way to earn money and keep going.

I decided to give it a try and bought a reseller hosting plan.

This reminded me of an old memory. When I was 16, I used to sell STD-PCO telecom services. I thought if I could do it back then, I could do it now.

In the next part of my story, I'll share how this new opportunity worked out for me. You'll see how my past experience helped me.

Just remember, when one way is blocked, there's always another one waiting. You just have to be brave enough to take it.

"In life's journey, remember you're not alone. Help comes unexpectedly, like Sharma Ji's credit or advice on reseller hosting. Keep pushing forward during tough times, your determination and resourcefulness will lead the way."

- **Manoj Dhanda**

CHAPTER 23

THE BEST RELIGION IN THE WORLD

Once I started on my new venture, the days began to take on a rhythm of their own. The initial days were full of hustle, making calls, sending SMSs, and marketing my services.

It was a race against time, but slowly and steadily, I began to see results.

Within a few days, I had managed to win over 14-15 customers. These customers were not just clients; they were a community - people I learned from and grew with. Their problems became my problems, and their success, my success. I engaged with them, addressed their issues, and worked relentlessly to provide effective solutions.

What happened next was beyond my expectations. My customers started sharing feedback. They praised the quality of my support and service. Their words, full of appreciation, were like a soothing balm to my tired spirit. "Your service is exceptional!" they said, their smiles speaking volumes.

Many shared that they had never experienced such prompt and effective assistance before. In a world where true service seemed like a forgotten art, they felt valued and cared for. These responses filled my heart with a sense of fulfillment that no amount of money could ever offer.

But they didn't stop there. They went on to say something that moved me deeply. They admired my communication skills and my approach to problem-solving. In their eyes, these were not just skills but a glimpse of my potential. They believed that with these abilities, I was destined for greatness in life.

This was a turning point in my journey. I realized that service, in its purest form, is more than just a transaction. It is a connection, a bridge between hearts. It's not about what we give or get, but about how we make others feel. It is the ultimate religion, a sacred path that leads to growth and fulfillment.

As we move forward in this journey, you will discover how these words of appreciation and faith shaped my vision and became the fuel for my relentless pursuit of success.

Always remember, my friends, it's not the grandeur of our actions but the love and sincerity within them that truly makes a difference. Every small act of service sows the seeds of big changes. So, let's keep serving, keep spreading the light, and create a world that is a little more kind, a little more connected.

"Find rhythm in hustle, community in clients, and joy in service. Remember, it's not just what we offer but how we connect that truly matters. Small acts can sow seeds of great changes - serve, connect, and make the world a little kinder."

- Manoj Dhanda

CHAPTER 24

10×10 ROOM–
MY FIRST OFFICE

Every single event in our lives happens for a reason. They come together like pieces of a puzzle, each playing its part in the grand scheme of things. For me, my journey so far, my experiences, my interactions, all pointed me in one direction.

It was time for me to step up and create something of my own. A spark ignited within me, and a determination kindled to create my very own hosting platform. Thus, in a humble 10x10 room, the story of **MICROHOST** began to unfold.

As the calendar pages turned, and the year 2010 rolled in, I found myself in the city of Noida. A city known as the 'Electronic City', a bustling hub for the software industry.

Here I was, a small-town boy, standing in the heart of Noida (Sector 18), with around 30 customers to my name.

Noida was a city full of possibilities, filled with new faces and fresh challenges. But there was a fire in my heart, a fire that was fueled by my dreams.

I was determined in my decision - no matter what, I had to keep moving forward.

And so, I did. With each passing day, my customer base began to grow.

From a modest 30, the number reached 100 within two months. It was as if the city was embracing me, supporting me in my journey.

Customers kept coming, and I continued serving them with all my heart.

Soon, the fruits of my relentless efforts began to show.

Money started flowing in, recurring money that was enough to support my family and myself.

The boy who once couldn't afford a meal was now supporting his family, all because of his hard work and the faith of his customers.

As we go ahead in this incredible journey. Let's discover together how a dream took shape in a small 10x10 room and evolved into a platform that served hundreds.

Remember, every big journey starts with a single step. It's not about how far we have to go, but how far we've come. So, let's keep moving forward, let's keep dreaming, because who knows, the next step might be the one that changes everything.

"Every great journey begins with a single step. It may start in a small room, with just an idea, but with determination and relentless effort, it can lead to incredible growth. The path may be challenging, new cities and new people may bring unforeseen obstacles, but with a steadfast mind, progress is inevitable. Keep serving, keep growing, and keep making a difference, because your journey matters not just to you, but to everyone you impact along the way."   **- Manoj Dhanda**

CHAPTER 25

I WAS ALONE

When you build something with your own hands, the pride you feel is beyond words. That's precisely how I felt about MICROHOST. It was like a tree I had planted and nurtured. It had grown into something significant, something real, something that was undeniably mine.

But in the midst of all this, I found myself alone. Success was there, but it felt like an empty room. Challenges came and went like waves on a shore. Each one stirred a storm of feelings inside me. Sometimes, I laughed at them, and sometimes, I cried.

In those quiet moments, my mind traveled back to the village I left behind. I remembered my friends, their faces fresh in my mind. I thought of our cricket matches in the narrow lanes, the sound of the bat hitting the ball still echoing in my ears. I missed the familiar joy of victory, the bitter taste of defeat.

I thought of my family - my parents, my siblings - who did everything they could for me. Those memories were like photographs in an old album, bringing a sweet pain to my heart.

Even after achieving so much, I felt alone. It was a strange feeling. Like standing in a crowd but feeling like you're the only one there. Life was teaching me something. It was a tough lesson, but it was important.

Amidst all this, I turned 22. It was not just another birthday. It was a milestone, a point in my journey that marked how far I had come, and how much farther I had to go.

Remember, life is not just about reaching the top, it's about the climb. It's about the lessons we learn, the moments we cherish, and the dreams we chase. So, let's keep climbing, let's keep dreaming, because every step we take is a part of our story. And every story is worth telling.

"Success is a journey of highs and lows that can often feel lonely. It's a path of personal growth and achievements, yet it can distance us from our roots. The most valuable lesson from this journey is that, despite success, we remain connected to our past and the memories that shaped us." **- Manoj Dhanda**

CHAPTER 26

A GREAT DISCOVERY!!!

The year 2013 marked a new chapter in my life - a chapter of togetherness. A wonderful woman named Kusum stepped into my world, and together, we tied the knots of a lifetime commitment, feeling as if life had finally found its place.

As we settled into our new life, Kusum one day asked, "Manoj, is this what you want to continue doing? Do you want to continue this journey alone?"

Her words echoed inside me, stirring a conversation with my own self. "No," my inner voice replied,

"No, I want to do something big. I want to do something significant"

Kusum Replied **"Then why are you doing it alone?"**

And Together, Kusum and I navigated this newfound revelation.

We realized that in order to bring about a significant change, to make a dent in the universe, we needed more than just our individual efforts. It was back then I realized that I could grow the business, but to thrive, I need my soldiers.

Kusum's words kept echoing in my mind, "To climb the mountain of success, we need a team. We need people. We need an office."

That was the moment of reckoning - the birth of a new vision.

I would no longer walk alone. Microhost was ready to evolve from a solitary journey into a team's journey.

From that day forward, we set out on the path of building our team. A team that wasn't merely a group of employees, but a family bound by the common thread of Microhost's mission.

I, who had been leading Microhost as a solo warrior, gradually saw the transformation around me. Each new member brought a piece of their own world, their unique experiences, their own dreams, and added it to the mosaic of Microhost.

As we continue this journey, walk with me as I share how a lone venture evolved into a collective dream, how a group of people transformed into a cohesive team, and how that team grew into a family despite the challenges.

Remember, the power of unity is far greater than individual strength. To create something big, something lasting, we need to join hands and move forward together. So, let's take a step forward, hand in hand, into the new chapter of this incredible journey.

"Great achievements are not born from individual effort alone, but from the collective strength of a committed team."

- Kusum Dhanda

CHAPTER 27

CHALLENGES, CASH FLOW, AND THE PURSUIT OF GROWTH

Each day in life is like a cricket match, throwing a new ball at us. Back in 2013, our Microhost family had just begun its innings, and we were facing some challenging deliveries.

There were days when the pitch seemed uncertain, and we didn't know how the ball would turn. But we had a strategy - to rely on our previous training, life lessons, and experiences. With that mindset, we picked up our bats and got ready to face the deliveries.

Managing a team felt like spinning many tops at the same time.

Keeping team members happy, paying their salaries on time, handling bills from data centers, and solving financial problems - every day felt like a tough over to play.

The money that we had to pay to suppliers started to pile up. Our pockets felt lighter, and it seemed like our hands were almost empty.

There were times when it felt like a heavy defeat. The lack of funds was like a constant bouncer, making us duck and dodge. We even had to borrow money, but our heads remained held high even in these difficult times.

Were we ready to give up? No. Even though the match was tough, our team spirit was strong, And our determination was our best foot forward. We weren't just a team; we were a family - supporting each other and facing every googly with a smile.

So, my friends, let's live this exciting match together. Let's see how every tough ball made us a better batsman, how every difficult over made us stronger, and how we learned to play every shot.

Remember, even the best batsman faces tough deliveries. They swing, they spin, but they never give up. Just like us.

Together, we will see how every tough time was just a stepping stone to victory, how the lack of money could not weaken our spirit, and how the desire to grow was not just about making the business big, but also about making ourselves better.

So, let's keep playing this exciting match, cherishing the fours and sixes, learning from the dot balls, and always ready for the next delivery. Because that's what we do.

We keep playing.

"Life is like a cricket match, each day presenting new challenges. Back in 2013, the Microhost family was in its early innings, strategizing, juggling finances, and maintaining team spirit. Even when money problems loomed, we never lost hope, tackling each obstacle with unity, perseverance, and a smile."

- Manoj Dhanda

Key Learnings for You

Handling Daily Challenges: Life is just like a cricket match, with each day presenting a new challenge. In 2013, we started our journey and faced many obstacles. Yet, we used our past experiences to tackle these challenges. It's essential to learn from our past and use it to deal with our present.

Juggling Multiple Tasks: Running a team is like juggling multiple balls. You have to keep your team happy, handle bills, and solve money problems. It's crucial to learn how to manage multiple tasks and keep everything in balance.

Staying Strong During Hard Times: There were times when we didn't have much money. We even had to borrow. But we didn't give up. We learned that it's essential to stay strong, support each other, and keep going, even when times are tough.

CHAPTER 28

JOURNEY OF COURAGE, DETERMINATION, AND SUCCESS

Imagine you are playing a Kabaddi match.

You have to keep going, tackling every opponent, learning from each move, trying new strategies, and all while you hold your breath.

It was the year 2015, and our Microhost family found itself in the middle of this intense game - facing team challenges, upscaling our game plan, learning from every move, and trying out new strategies.

In the midst of this thrilling match, we were gifted with a bundle of joy – Shaurya. His arrival filled our hearts with immense joy. But it also brought along a big question. A question that resonated in my mind, "When Shaurya grows up and asks me what I do, what answer will I give him?"

While I pondered over this question, our cash flow problem still lingered. I realized that our main issue was that we were deeply invested in technology, yet our sales figures were not matching up. Without strong sales, we struggled to attract new customers, and our cash flow continued to decline.

Then, I heard a voice inside me, like the whistle of a referee, signaling me to make my move. It was time for me to rise, take action, and change our game plan. So, I rolled up my sleeves and dedicated the next eight months to focused marketing efforts.

We put Microhost out there, like a daring kabaddi player ready to make a raid.

We advertised on the same TV and radio channels where we used to watch big companies making their mark.

As time went by, our efforts started bearing fruit. More and more customers started recognizing us, just like spectators cheering for their favorite player.

Our cash flow problem started easing up as the customer base increased, and Microhost started becoming a trusted name.

Just like a player winning the hearts of his audience, we started gaining recognition in the industry. The applause grew louder, and our hearts swelled with pride.

Let's dive deeper into this thrilling journey. Let's see how we faced every opponent, learned from each move, and came up with winning strategies. Remember, every good player faces tough competitors. They struggle, they learn, but they never give up. Just like us.

So, let's continue this exciting match, cherishing the victories, learning from the losses, and always ready for the next move. Because that's what we do. We keep playing.

"In life's journey, courage is the compass, determination is the engine, and success is the destination. Don't fear challenges, embrace them, as they fuel your drive to push forward and ignite your desire to become better."   **- Manoj Dhanda**

CHAPTER 29

MAKING INDIA'S FIRST CLOUD PLATFORM

We were like a small star in the huge world of the internet, but, like that small star, Microhost started to shine brighter each day.

To make our mark, we organized India's first-ever blogging event. We received an overwhelming response, with over a thousand bloggers registering and about 500 to 600 attending our event. This event made Microhost's name even more well-known, as it became a topic of conversation everywhere.

However, during this time, we identified a big need. People needed cloud services, but none of the big companies providing them were from India.

This realization made me firm in my decision. We were determined to create our own cloud service, the first one in India. We started understanding the problems that other cloud companies faced: they were complicated to use, expensive, and lacked good customer support.

With this in mind, we started our journey to create India's first-ever cloud platform. Yes, it was a big task, but we were ready for the challenge.

Let's add a new chapter in India's digital story - a story of taking risks, not giving up, and, most importantly, a story of India's success.

Remember, in the vast sky full of opportunities, we are not just any star; we are a shining star, leading the way for others to follow.

"Every challenge in life is an opportunity for you to shine. Remember, even the smallest star can illuminate the darkest night, so believe in your potential, and be the beacon of inspiration for others." **- Manoj Dhanda**

CHAPTER 30

TURNING DREAMS INTO REALITY

It took two years of hard work, day and night, in the timeless world of cloud computing. And after those two years, in 2018, Microhost finally transformed from Microhost to Microhost Cloud.

India finally had its own, first-ever cloud platform!!!

After the launch, I ran my first marketing campaign and headed home...

As I was telling Kusum about the launch and wondering what the response would be, my phone rang, and a voice on the other end said, "Sir, something amazing has happened!" I quickly asked, "What happened? First, tell me what you did.' They replied, "Sir, there has been a flood of people on our website, asking numerous questions."

I swiftly grabbed my laptop, logged in, and, to my delight, saw that 700 to 800 people had registered on our platform.

Tears of joy filled my eyes, but there was also a sense of fear because we hadn't fully prepared the infrastructure as we should have.

We realized the need to scale up, and within two hours, we had to put up a 'Sold Out' banner on our platform and requested customers to place their orders at a later time.

And so, we got to work, striving to make our platform better, expanding our capacity, and setting up a scalable infrastructure. Because on that day, it was proven that what we had done was indeed needed by the country. There was a demand for our business course, and people had placed their trust in us.

The fact that 800 individuals showed us their love and had faith in us was the reason we kept pushing forward.

"Dream big, work hard, and be patient. Your vision, combined with hard work, can create impactful and transformational change."
                                                    - Manoj Dhanda

CHAPTER (31)

LEARNING TO SCALING

And as we enabled the platform again, customers started pouring in, orders started flowing, and the demand was beyond our expectations.

Recurring cash flow started to come in, and it felt like we had achieved something significant. Life seemed to be going well. But then, the next challenge arose—scaling the business.

We realized the need for processes and systems within the business. We had never learned or been taught about running a business before, but now was the time to learn.

I immersed myself in business coaching, implemented processes, and established systems. A corporate culture began to take shape.

"Scaling a business goes beyond just increasing revenue. It's about understanding the importance of robust systems, processes, and a company culture. Take continuous learning, as it can transform your business from a successful startup to a thriving enterprise."   **- Manoj Dhanda**

CHAPTER  32

BEST REALIZATION OF MY LIFE

Everything was going well. The company was profitable, and I personally indulged in luxuries like buying a new house in the best society of the city and a car.

It was a time when it seemed like I could have anything I wanted, but as time went on, I began to realize that I was not satisfied with my life.

I questioned myself, "Is this all I am here for?

Is my sole purpose just to make money?

Will life pass by in this manner?"

"The true richness of life isn't measured by material possessions but by the fulfillment of our deepest purpose. Accumulating wealth can bring comfort, but it's the quest for meaning that truly satisfies the soul. Never let life pass by in the pursuit of just money. Seek your purpose."
                                                    - Manoj Dhanda

CHAPTER 33

MAKING A DIFFERENCE DURING THE COVID-19 PANDEMIC

And during this time, the COVID-19 pandemic struck.

I witnessed my country in distress, with people running helter-skelter and a prevailing sense of helplessness. It reminded me of a time when I, too, was alone, crying, and struggling.

And I thought about what I could do….

The entire team had shifted to working from home as companies were transitioning to remote work.

Some people reached out to me, asking for VPN services and Tally on Cloud. They asked if I could provide those services, and I replied, "Absolutely, we will do it." I saw this as an opportunity to help Indian businesses in difficult times and empower remote work.

My team and I worked tirelessly, day and night, and within four days, we launched the VPN and Tally on Cloud services.

"In times of crisis, we discover our true capacity to make a difference. As we faced the COVID-19 pandemic, it wasn't about business, but about empowering and aiding others in distress. When you shift the focus from 'I' to 'we', you can turn challenges into opportunities for positive change."

- Manoj Dhanda

CHAPTER 34

PARTNERING WITH "ATMA NIRBHAR BHARAT"

It was a proud feeling that we were doing something for our country, something for the businesses of our nation.

And at that moment, I understood the true joy that comes from serving customers, bringing forth new innovations, and effective positive changes.

It's not just about making money; it's about serving others.

I made a commitment that whatever I do from now on, it will be for technology, for business, and for my country.

I vowed that I would never let anyone be alone in their struggles.

I would stand by their side and help them in difficult times.

But I had another challenge in front of me.

The foreign companies had dominated the market in my own country.

They had all the marketing funds and large teams. However, I had the determination, passion, and courage to make Indian Cloud the market leader.

I envisioned a digitally independent India, free from the clutches of those foreign companies who were taking the wealth of our nation outside its borders.

During that time, the Honorable Prime Minister announced the concept of "Atma Nirbhar Bharat" (Self-Reliant India) and emphasized the importance of being vocal for locals.

This resonated with me deeply. I gained more courage and determination to do something for the nation, for Indian businesses.

I decided to align myself with this vision and believed that the entire nation was with me.

> "Serving a nation and its businesses brings true joy. Let's unite to build a digitally independent India, be vocal for local, and embrace the vision of an Atmanirbhar Bharat. Let our dedication create positive change and keep the wealth within our borders"
>
> **- Manoj Dhanda**

CHAPTER 35

THIS WORLD IS MINE

I recalled the line from my Guruji, "Manoj, Yah Duniya Tumhari To Hai" (This world belongs to you as much as it belongs to me).

And from within, I heard a voice saying, "Manoj, this world is yours." I found my vision, and along with it, I found the mission of my life.

From that moment, my mission was not only to build a successful business but also to contribute to the growth and development of my country, to empower Indian businesses, and to make a positive impact on the nation's economy.

In order to move forward with this mission, I needed to become stronger.

I had to learn a lot, so I attended various training sessions, worked on myself extensively, and practiced meditation.

I delved deep into my soul and identified habits and mindsets that were not serving me well. I made the decision to remove them from my life completely.

To embark on this mission, I needed courage, consistent effort, and an unshakable resolve.

"Believe the world is yours. Cultivate resilience, embrace challenges as opportunities, and invest in self-improvement. Let go of limiting beliefs, approach life with courage and consistent effort. Make a positive impact, contribute to growth, and trust in your journey. The world awaits your potential."

- Manoj Dhanda

CHAPTER 36

ENRICHMENT BEGINS WITHIN

It took me 1.5 years to transform myself, and then I started roaring like a lion. I made up my mind that I would not back down from any challenge that came my way.

I was determined to do everything it took to make my mission successful, not just for myself but also for my organization and my country.

I felt a deep connection with my soul, mind, heart, and every cell of my body.

During this journey, I learned the most important lesson of my life: if you want to achieve something significant in life, be prepared to put in the effort required, just like a player who trains hard throughout the year before entering the match.

I had put in that hard work and preparation.

Transform yourself, then run like a lion. Embrace challenges fearlessly and commit to success. Connect with your soul, mind, and heart. Learn the vital lesson: to achieve greatness, put in the necessary effort and preparation. Your journey begins within.

- Manoj Dhanda

CHAPTER 37

UTHO: A New Mission

And now it was time to give Microhost a new name because the purpose had been established.

The purpose was to uplift every person who had faced defeat in life, every business that was operating in fear, every area where growth was stagnant, and the entire Indian cloud infrastructure still dominated by foreign companies.

I had to uplift them, reshape them, and make them grow. The name of the purpose was given: UTHO, which means "RISE."

With this, Microhost transformed into UTHO, fueled by new determination and immense energy. A fire ignited in my heart, knowing that the time had come to take action and uplift the nation.

When businesses do well, our people do well, and when our people do well, our whole country does well. It's like everyone climbing together to reach greater heights, building a brighter future for us all.

Don't let fear hold you back. Trust in yourself and have the courage to take that leap of faith. Remember, every journey begins with a single step, just as UTHO emerges with a mission to empower those who've faced defeat, businesses in fear, and stagnant areas, transforming them by uplifting, reshaping, and igniting growth. **- Manoj Dhanda**

CHAPTER 38

EMPOWERING AND RESHAPING THE TEAM

Life brought me to a turning point, where I initiated this journey. It felt like it was time to restructure everything for the mission and align with the vision.

We spoke to some customers, gathered feedback about our current services, and discovered areas that needed improvement.

We began restructuring the team internally, focusing on creating a customer-centric attitude, enhancing performance, and adding value to the cloud journey.

Regrettably, we had to let go of those in our company who couldn't meet these standards, despite our efforts and support.

We valued them, showed them love, and bid them farewell.

We needed a team structure and individuals who would prioritize the customer, think about technology, performance, and how to transform the cloud journey.

"Reshape. Adapt. Prioritize customers. Build a winning team aligned with your mission. Let go. Embrace room for growth.

- Manoj Dhanda

CHAPTER 39

LEARNING FROM MISTAKES AND EMBRACING FORGIVENESS

The journey continued with renewed purpose, and we built a team aligned with the vision of UTHO.

With this, we reached out to all our customers through email, acknowledging our mistakes, apologizing, and expressing our appreciation.

Our customers rewarded us for being vulnerable, as a result, we received a flood of orders, and many previous customers returned.

This journey taught us that making mistakes is inevitable, but not correcting them and accepting them is an even bigger mistake.

Whenever you make a mistake in life, accept it, apologize, and seize the opportunity to make it right. Believe me, life will change.

"Learn from mistakes, embrace forgiveness. Apologize, correct, and grow. Service is the key to lasting success when given with the right attitude."

- Manoj Dhanda

"You will never run out of service if you have an attitude of giving service." **- Manoj Dhanda**

CHAPTER 40

IMPOSSIBLE SAYS "I M POSSIBLE"

After all these experiences, we faced our biggest challenge: providing better performance at a lower price. It seemed impossible at times to be at par with the foreign companies as I didn't have the required resources.

However, instead of using the shortage of resources as an excuse, I took complete ownership of making the seemingly impossible a reality.

I dedicated myself day and night, and after a few days of hard work, I managed to reduce the price by 60% compared to foreign companies while delivering double the performance.

"Ruk jana nahi, tu kahi tu kahi har ke, kanton pe chalke milenge saye bahar ke.

(Don't give up, keep going no matter what, and you'll find shelter beyond the challenges).

Today, I am filled with joy as I share that we have achieved victory in reliability and performance, all while offering cost-effective cloud services and providing better customer support akin to a mother's love. We have done it all.

I take pride in stating that UTHO now routes 80% of India's cloud telephone calls through our services.

With this, we empower every individual and every business.

Whenever anyone needs assistance, they can contact their service provider, their bank, or any relevant person and find a solution to their problem.

"Redefining performance and price, we never stop; we overcome every obstacle. Delivering value and excellence. UTHO brings reliability, performance, and cost-effective solutions, empowering every individual and business. You have the power to create change"   **- Manoj Dhanda**

To Be Continued...